This book has been published in cooperation with Evans Publishing Group.

© Evans Brothers Limited 2010
This edition published under license from Evans Brothers Limited.

Published in the United States by
Amicus
P.O. Box 1329, Mankato, Minnesota 56002

Printed in China by New Era Printing Co.Ltd

Library of Congress Cataloging-in-Publication Data
Senker, Cath.
  Construction careers / by Cath Senker.
      p. cm. -- (In the workplace)
  Includes bibliographical references and index.
  Summary: "Describes jobs in the construction and building trades. Includes information on equipment operators, carpenters, electricians, inspectors, and more, covering their responsibilities and training needed. Also includes profiles of workers in the industry"
  -- Provided by publisher.
  ISBN 987-1-60753-089-3 (library binding)
  1. Building--Vocational guidance--Juvenile literature. I. Title.
  TH159.S46 2011
  690.023--dc22

                                                                     2009054193

Editor and picture researcher: Patience Coster
Designer: Guy Callaby

The author would like to thank the following for their help in producing this book: Liz Bland; Tim Bulpin; Ruthie Crawshaw; Claire Haigh; Martin Heather; Stuart Lynn; Lucía Raso Mateo; Darren Smith; Simon Swainson; Dennis Sweet; Anthony Wiltshire.

We are grateful to the following for permission to reproduce photographs:
Alamy 6 (Peter Casolino), 9 (Stock Connection), 11 (Chris Cooper-Smith), 12 (Greenshoots Communications), 14 (Philip Wolmuth), 20 (Lourens Smak), 21 (Leslie Garland Picture Library), 22 (David J. Green – electrical), 23 (Sciencephotos), 24 (Photofusion Picture Library), 25 (Bubbles Photolibrary), 26 (David J. Green – work themes), 27 (James Quine), 28 (Mike Goldwater), 29 (67photo), 31 (Lawrence Wee), 32 (Bildagentur Hamburg), 33 (Maximilian Stock Ltd/ Phototake), 38 (Eric James), 39 (Geogphotos), cover and 40 (Archimage), 41 (qaphotos. com), 43 (Justin Kase zsixz); Corbis 19 (Construction Photography); Getty 30 (John Zoiner), 36 (Siri Stafford); iStockphoto 7, 8, 10, 13, 15, 16, 17, 18, 34, 35, 37, 42.

05 10
PO1568

IN THE
WORKPLACE

Construction Careers

CATH SENKER

amicus
mankato, minnesota

Contents

Working in Construction

A job in construction could allow you to work on all kinds of building projects. You might be helping to construct a brand-new housing development, a state-of-the-art sports stadium, or an impressive bridge. You could even be restoring historic buildings to their former glory.

The construction industry is very important for people and the economy, providing much-needed housing, offices, and public buildings. The way it operates is significant for the environment, too—the construction of environmentally-friendly buildings can help to reduce carbon dioxide emissions.

A WORLD OF OPPORTUNITY

A variety of businesses are involved in the construction industry. You might work for an international company engaged in giant construction projects worldwide or a small family-run business maintaining local homes. You could be a self-employed craft worker, for example a cabinetmaker, taking on jobs for builders or individuals.

HANDY HINT
The construction industry is encouraged to adopt environmental standards laid down by oranizations such as the U.S. Green Building Council. If you keep up-to-date with new sustainable building methods, you'll be an asset to the industry.

A rare example of a female construction worker. A tiny proportion of people working in the construction trades are women, although more work in the professional and technical sectors.

A contractor carries out a site inspection. Large numbers of skilled people are required to plan, organize, and inspect construction jobs.

Many different types of jobs are available, including professional, technical, and hands-on work. You could be designing an arts center or using specialized skills as a CAD operator, bricklayer, or carpenter.

In construction, you can start at any level and work your way up to a senior job or gain enough experience to set up your own business. Although most people in the construction industry are men, there are opportunities for women, too. For example, in the United States in 2007, 1 percent of employed women worked in natural resources, construction, and maintenance occupations—that's around 680,000 women.

FINDING A JOB

Most construction workers start by getting a job with a contractor who provides on-the-job training, but formal apprentice programs are also available. Apprenticeships for construction laborers require a high school diploma or equivalent.

LOCATION AND HOURS

Your job could be local or anywhere in the country. Construction work can take you abroad, too. In this sector, you should be prepared to travel, and at times you may have to live away from home for a while. Regarding working hours, you'll generally work a normal workweek, but it is likely that you will have to work overtime as well. Sometimes you'll need to work long hours to meet deadlines.

RIGHT FOR THE JOB?

Large construction projects bring together teams of workers, so you need to be able to work well with other people. If you'd prefer to work alone, you can be self-employed and take on small jobs. Many construction tasks require strength and stamina, so you should be fit and healthy. You'll often be working outdoors or in half-finished buildings, in all weather and in difficult conditions. In jobs such as scaffolding and roofing, it helps to not be afraid of heights. You'll have to be aware of health and safety issues—building sites can be dangerous places.

Preparing for Construction

At the start of a construction job, laborers demolish the old structures and prepare for the new building. First on the scene are the outdoor workers, including demolition contractors, equipment operators, and scaffolders.

You can train for these types of employment on the job—a good way is to do an apprenticeship. You'll be given extensive training on the aspects of your job as well as safety, because you may come into contact with hazardous materials, and the work itself can be risky.

DEMOLITION CONTRACTORS

Much construction work takes place on brownfield sites—locations with buildings that were used previously but are no longer needed. To prepare the construction site, demolition contractors dismantle the unwanted structures.

Smashing down buildings may sound easy, but it's a skilled job. First, you erect fences around the site. Then you remove any reusable fixtures and fittings. After that, you take away doors and windows. Once hand demolition is completed, experienced contractors use special cutting equipment to demolish the structure safely. They may even need to use explosives. It's a dramatic moment when the structure finally comes tumbling down!

TO WORK IN CONSTRUCTION, YOU WILL NEED

● *physical fitness*

● *good manual skills*

● *an awareness of safety issues*

Demolition work requires the skilled use of large machinery, such as this crane.

KNOCKOUT JOB

For this job, you should be capable of working at heights and in all weather conditions. You'll need good manual skills and should be able to carry and use heavy equipment. Bear in mind that you'll be working in dusty, dirty, and noisy conditions. You'll have to wear a range of protective gear, including goggles, a helmet, and ear protection. Sometimes, you'll require breathing equipment, too.

Here, the Kaiser Hospital in Hawaii is demolished using controlled explosions. The building collapses amid billowing dust.

FINDING A JOB

You can start out as a general construction laborer to gain experience. You'll do basic tasks such as moving building materials and helping to lay drains, as well as operating equipment such as cement mixers.

HANDY HINT

Outdoor construction jobs can be exciting and are great if you want to avoid a nine-to-five office existence. But it's worth knowing that construction workers are prone to health problems because of the hard physical work they do. Common health issues include back pain from lifting and carrying heavy objects, skin and breathing problems from dust and toxic substances used in construction, and hearing impairment due to noise levels and vibration.

CONSTRUCTION EQUIPMENT OPERATORS

If you like the idea of driving and operating massive diggers and dump trucks on a construction site, this job could be for you. As an equipment operator, you operate all kinds of vehicles, including bulldozers, excavators, and cranes. One day, you might be using an enormous 360-degree excavator to shift huge quantities of soil and rock. Another day, you could be using a static tower crane to lift heavy building materials into position. You might also operate machines required for the building process, such as concrete mixers and rollers for flattening out the work area.

As well as working on site, you'll drive these monster vehicles to and from building sites—a skilled job in itself. You'll also need to carry out regular safety checks on the equipment.

IN THE CAB

Working conditions on the construction site may be dusty, muddy, noisy, cold, or hot. You'll mostly be working in the cab of the vehicle, sometimes at a great height, using levers and switches to control the machine.

TO BECOME A CONSTRUCTION EQUIPMENT OPERATOR, YOU WILL NEED

●

some knowledge of construction equipment

●

the ability to concentrate hard

●

the ability to work safely and responsibly

The best way to train to work with bulldozers and other heavy equipment is to take an apprenticeship.

Martin: Equipment Operator

"I've been driving and operating [construction equipment] for 18 years. When I left school, I wasn't sure what to do. I tried mechanics and then decided on the building trade. I tried stonemasonry and then became interested in machines. I found employment on a building site and learned to operate [machines] on the job. Nowadays, you need some training before you start operating the machines.

Today, large machines are computer controlled. This driver uses a computer system to guide most of the crane's actions.

"I work a nine-hour day. I'm qualified to operate many different kinds of equipment. On a typical day, I could be using a forward-tipping dump truck, a 360-degree excavator, or a telescopic forklift. These machines can move vast quantities of material— the excavator can [move] a load of up to 30 tons! I do various kinds of jobs. I might be laying down pipes underground or preparing roads for blacktopping.

"Operating [equipment] is great on a cold and wet day because I'm nice and dry in the cab. It's satisfying using large machines, doing a big job on a big scale. At the end of the day, you can see the results of your work. It can be a bit lonely, though. The other site workers are in a team, while I'm in my own little world in the cab.

"If you're interested in being [an equipment] operator, there are several options. It's best to come into the industry and try it out."

TO BECOME A SCAFFOLDER, YOU WILL NEED

●

to be an excellent team worker

●

an excellent sense of balance and no fear of heights

●

physical fitness

UP ON THE SCAFFOLDING

Not afraid of heights? Scaffolders put up scaffolding for new construction projects and to enable maintenance work on existing structures. You could be erecting scaffolding for housing, a bridge, stands in a sports stadium, or even a film set. You'll usually work outdoors, although there are some indoor jobs.

Creating scaffolding involves joining tubes together to form a framework and attaching scaffold boards onto it. You'll need to be able to take measurements accurately and use a variety of hand tools, such as ratchets to attach the tubes together and a level to check that the boards are horizontal.

This scaffolder uses a level while putting up the scaffolding for a water and sewage treatment plant in Ghana, West Africa.

Safety is crucial. You have to keep yourself and your fellow workers safe while working at great heights and ensure that the scaffolding is secure to avoid causing any harm to passersby. This job requires a high level of concentration. It's tough physical work. You'll need to be fit and strong to climb up and down ladders while carrying heavy equipment.

Tim: Scaffolder

"I've been working as a scaffolder for 10 years. When I started out, I didn't know anything about the job. I began by doing basic tasks, such as fetching scaffolding and carrying it up the ladders. I worked my way up, and now I'm a supervisor.

"I work for a medium-size scaffolding company, and we're subcontracted to work on different sites. The jobs vary—we might do three or four small jobs in a day, or we could be working on a big project for a while. I work an eight-hour day, but I have to travel to work, and the job could be a two-hour drive away.

"Many people [try] scaffolding work and give up after just a couple of weeks. It's not for the faint-hearted. The job is very physical. There could be 12 tons of gear to move into position, and you might have to [move it three times] to get it there. That's like [moving] 36 tons of material! Building sites are noisy and dirty. When you take down scaffolding, it's covered in sand and cement from the construction work, so you go home absolutely filthy at the end of the day.

"As a scaffolder, you get fit, and you become so used to carrying heavy materials that you barely notice it. It's a steady job, with good prospects of progressing to supervisory levels. It's become a respected profession, too. Other workers on site appreciate that you're doing a tough job."

Scaffolding has been erected to enable the construction of apartments.

Putting Up Buildings

After the foundations are laid, a host of craftspeople help to put up the new building: Bricklayers construct the walls, carpenters build the wooden structures, and roofers create the roof. Other specialists play their part, too, such as floor layers, glaziers, and tilers.

As with the jobs in chapter 1, to do the jobs shown here, you can train while you're working or take an apprenticeship, which allows you to work and to study the trade as well.

LAY IT ON WITH A TROWEL

Bricklayers build and maintain the outside and inside walls of all kinds of buildings. As a bricklayer, you use hammers to cut bricks or stones to the right shape. You spread mortar with a trowel, and then you lay the bricks accurately in position.

Stonemasons specialize in working with stone. Some masons use hand and power tools to carve stones for new buildings and to restore old buildings. Others build stone walls or repair stonework. Some stonemasons design monuments and memorials.

BUILDING SKILLS

Bricklayers and stonemasons mostly work outdoors in all weather, and the conditions can be dirty and dusty. You'll often have to stand or kneel for long periods, and the work can be repetitive. You'll need to be fit to lift heavy materials. It's important to be able to follow plans accurately and to have a good eye for checking that the walls are perfectly straight.

MAIN TASKS: STONEMASON

- *following design instructions*
- *carving stone*
- *using tools to create a finish on the stone*
- *building stone walls*
- *repairing damaged stonework*

FINDING A JOB
There are no particular qualifications required to start as a bricklayer or stonemason, but employers usually hire people who have some experience. It is useful to work as a laborer on a building site first. Once in a job, you may be able to train as a bricklayer or stonemason.

Bricklayers have to work fast but accurately. This bricklayer checks that the wall he is constructing is perfectly straight.

Bricklaying is a tough job physically. This bricklayer has to bend down for long periods while building up the wall.

Dennis: Bricklayer

"I've been a bricklayer for about 20 years. First I went to [a technical] college and took a two-year bricklaying course. Then I went to work for a friend who was a contractor, and I received [excellent] training.

"Bricklayers usually work an eight-hour day. It's very demanding on the body because you're constantly lifting bricks, bending, and twisting. I found that the job suited me, though. Once I'd gained experience, I became self-employed.

"When you work for yourself, you can either do piece work and be paid according to the number of bricks you lay, or you can work for an hourly rate. If you're experienced and can lay around 600 bricks a day, it can be better to go for piece work. You can lay all your bricks for the day and go home. The downside is that you can't work when the weather is really bad, and sometimes you have to make a month's pay last for six weeks.

"After 10 years of working for myself, I took a job as a supervisor. Now I have a guaranteed regular wage.

"If you're considering working as a bricklayer, it's worth taking a course to get qualified. When you're looking for work, check that you'll be trained by an expert tradesperson so that you can progress in the industry."

WORKING WITH WOOD

Carpenters and joiners make and repair wooden structures, such as staircases, doors, floorboards, and window frames. Bench joiners work in workshops making parts; site carpenters fit the parts; and shopfitters specialize in giving stores a makeover. Other carpenters make wooden forms for concrete structures, such as the pillars in multistory parking ramps. The wooden structures hold the freshly poured concrete in place until it has hardened. As well as working on new buildings, carpenters help to improve existing buildings, working on expansions or repairing woodwork.

Naturally, to be a carpenter, you'll have to have a love of wood, and you'll have to be comfortable handling power tools such as sanders and jigsaws. You'll need excellent manual skills for using hammers and chisels, too. A knowledge of math is vital for taking accurate measurements and calculating angles; sometimes you'll need to figure out how to fit wood into awkward spaces. Wood is heavy, so you'll need to be strong to move the materials.

Working conditions can be challenging. You'll frequently be working on a dirty building site in all weather, often in an uncomfortable position. Carpenters have to bend, kneel, crouch, and stand for a long time. You'll often need to wear protective gear, such as goggles and ear protection. The workshop environment can be unpleasant, too—the air is full of wood dust.

BE YOUR OWN BOSS

You can gain experience in different types of carpentry and progress to become a supervisor. Alternatively, with a few years of experience under your belt, you could become self-employed.

TO BECOME A CARPENTER, YOU WILL NEED
- *good manual skills*
- *to be able to follow plans*
- *physical fitness*

This carpenter uses a machine called a router with a diamond-shaped device clamped to it. It allows him to cut a diamond-shaped inlay in the wood.

Some carpenters specialize in one area of carpentry—this woodworker makes cabinets.

Stuart: Carpenter

"I've been a carpenter for about eight years. I started out doing a two-year apprenticeship—I worked four days a week and went to [technical] college one day a week. Afterward, I worked for a company for a year and then became self-employed.

"I mostly work in a team doing attic conversions. We put steel beams in the joists, insulate them, and then put the floor down. Then we build the dormer window, first creating the side walls and joists, and then applying the new roof. We put in the internal walls and put up plasterboard inside. Then we cut the stairwell and put in the stairs. Sometimes I lay a wood floor.

"The work can be tough. I'm on my knees a lot of the time, often in tight spaces, so it can be uncomfortable and tiring. It's a [great] trade to learn, though. Carpentry can be well paid—it's usually better if you're self-employed.

"If you're thinking about a job in carpentry, decide whether you'd rather work in a workshop as a joiner or as an on-site carpenter. I'd advise you to study as much as you can, which will give you better job opportunities."

ON THE ROOF

Once the structure of a building is in place, it requires a roof. This is where the roofers come in. Roofers construct and repair roofs on all types of buildings, including houses, offices, public buildings, and shopping centers.

There are two main kinds of roofs—flat and pitched (sloped). You can work on both kinds or focus on one type. There are different kinds of roofing materials, too, including tiles, slate, asphalt shingles, and sheet materials. Again, you can train to use various materials or decide to focus on one type. You'll use different tools depending on the materials you're working with.

LAYING ROOFS

Roof slaters and tilers lay new tiles and slates or replace broken ones. You'll learn to lay the slates or tiles in rows and to cut the end and corner pieces to fit. Most modern roofs are composed of asphalt shingles, which require laying down a waterproof "felt" layer first. The shingles are then laid over it in large sections, or squares.

A roofer lays shingles on a building, the final part of a roofing job. The shingles form a protective layer that keeps out rainwater.

MAIN TASKS: ROOFER
●
laying new roofs
●
repairing existing roofs
●
installing weatherproof shields
●
installing roof sheeting
●
waterproofing masonry

SPECIAL ROOFS

You could work on some extraordinary types of roofs. In a conservation job, you might repair the roof of a historic home or mansion. You might even learn the old-fashioned craft of thatching. Today, a small but increasing number of buildings have "green" roofs. After installing a waterproof lining, you place layers of soil on top so that plants and grass can be grown there.

ON TOP OF THE WORLD

Clearly, to be a roofer, you'll need to be happy to climb ladders and scaffolding, often carrying tools and materials, and to work at heights. In this potentially dangerous occupation, you often need to wear a harness for safety. This is a physically demanding job, especially in hot, cold, or windy weather. The higher up you are, the harsher the conditions can be. It's worth knowing that some roofing materials, such as roof sheeting, are hard to handle.

As this is an outdoor job, you'll work during daylight hours, and there may be overtime. You'll need to move from site to site for work, and you may have to spend some time away from home.

WHERE WILL I BE?
In all the outdoor jobs, you can work your way up to supervisory or managerial levels within a company. With several years of experience, you can choose to set up your own business.

This roofer is helping to construct the roof of a new subway tunnel —a huge roofing job.

EXPERTS IN THE HOUSE

How about specializing as a floor installer, glazier, or tiler? This sort of work offers a lot of job satisfaction, but it can be challenging. Although perhaps not as physically demanding as being a roofer or bricklayer, you will need to carry heavy materials and sometimes work in difficult conditions.

ON THE FLOOR

Floor installers lay different kinds of flooring, such as carpet, vinyl, tile, and hardwood. You could be putting down rubber flooring in a factory, stone tiles in a kitchen, or carpets in a private home. You may choose to become an expert in one type of flooring.

As a floor installer, you first measure the area and draw up a plan or diagram. You also measure the flooring material. It's crucial to be able to make accurate plans and follow them carefully. The calculations can be quite complicated—floors do not always have straight edges, especially in older buildings, but the floor must have no gaps. Then you prepare the surface to ensure it is clean, level, and dry. You cut the flooring material to the exact measurements, which requires good coordination.

IN THE WINDOW

Glaziers work with glass and other window materials, such as plastic glass substitutes. They install and repair windows in homes and for businesses. For this job, you need to be able to calculate accurately and work carefully because glass is fragile and can be dangerous. Awareness of health and safety is crucial.

A flooring expert uses an electric jigsaw to lay a wooden parquet floor in the living room of a house.

WHERE WILL I BE?

It's possible to enter all the building jobs in this chapter as a trainee or apprentice and work your way up. With experience, you can move into a supervisory position, become self-employed, or set up your own business.

This job can involve work at all hours—glass may get broken at any time of day or night. You could be called out in an emergency to repair the glass window of a shop front that has been smashed in the middle of the night.

ON THE TILES

Tilers tile the walls and floors of all kinds of buildings to create durable, easy-to-clean surfaces. You could be tiling in homes, supermarkets, or hospitals. You prepare the surface, spread adhesive, and lay the tiles. Some tilers undertake artistic work, creating decorative tiling. As well as having excellent manual skills to lay the tiles accurately, it's useful to have some design and color sense for advising customers.

These glaziers use a suction clamp to position a sheet of glass in a new shopping center. Glaziers often have to work at heights.

Inside Jobs

Once the building has been constructed, a variety of craftspeople arrive to carry out the interior jobs. They include electricians, plumbers, plasterers, painters, and paperhangers. A sensible way of training for these kinds of jobs is to become an apprentice.

BRIGHT SPARKS: ELECTRICIANS

Electricians install and check wiring systems in all types of buildings. As an electrician, you could be working in homes, in factories, or out on the streets, fixing lighting and traffic systems.

This is a highly skilled job. You need to be adept with your hands and able to use a variety of tools, such as drills and screwdrivers. You'll need to be highly safety conscious to work with electricity and know the regulations governing the installation of electrical systems. It's important to be capable in math, technology, and science—particularly physics —to understand the principles of electricity and to work out wiring diagrams.

It's helpful to have an interest in new technology, too. New installation methods are continually being developed. Many local governments and businesses are trying to reduce their electricity use and are investing in new ways to light, heat, and ventilate their buildings. As an electrical apprentice, you can learn how to work with solar, wind, and geothermal energy systems. Increasingly, electricians are expected to be proficient in computers, for example, to work on computer-controlled building management systems. If you keep up with the latest developments, you will be greatly in demand.

An electrician tests for live wires while installing a new electricity meter.

TO BECOME AN ELECTRICIAN, YOU WILL NEED
●
normal color vision to differentiate between different-colored wires
●
physical fitness
●
good communication skills

This electrician wires a ceiling fixture in a house. Electricians need to be good at problem-solving to identify faults in wiring systems.

ON THE JOB
The conditions vary depending on where you work. You could be in a warm home updating the wiring system or on a ladder on a cold day repairing a street light. In general, the job involves a lot of bending, stretching, and working in cramped situations. You may also have to work at heights. Sometimes, you'll work alone, although on a big project, you'll be part of a team.

MAIN TASKS: ELECTRICIAN
●
installing control equipment and fuse boxes
●
putting in wiring systems
●
connecting wiring to sockets, light fixtures, and appliances
●
testing wiring systems
●
diagnosing problems and making repairs where necessary

HANDY HINT
It's useful if you are able to work flexibly to fit in with customers' needs and prepared to work in the evenings and on weekends. In some jobs, you may be on call 24 hours a day in case of an emergency.

PLUMBERS

As a plumber, you carry out a wide range of tasks to install and maintain sanitation, heating, and hot and cold water systems in all kinds of buildings. Your work may involve fitting the pipes for bathtubs and toilets or laying drainage pipes. HVAC specialists install and repair heating or air-conditioning systems. If you work on gas systems, you'll fit and maintain gas appliances such as central heating boilers.

The work involves cutting, bending, and joining pipes made from different materials, such as copper, aluminum, and plastic. You use a variety of power and hand tools, such as cutters and welding equipment. As well as being practical and dexterous, you should also be able to follow technical drawings. It's important to be thorough, too. Once the installation or repair is complete, you need to check that everything is working properly.

Plumbers regularly have to squeeze themselves into tight corners. This plumber is installing a new bathroom.

WHAT'S IN THE PIPELINE?

At times, you may have to work in uncomfortable, cold, or dusty conditions. Dealing with blocked drains or toilets can be extremely smelly and unpleasant. You could be working all hours if you are on call for emergencies. If there's a gas or water leak, there's no time to lose. On the plus side, it is possible to become self-employed and earn a high salary. Well-qualified plumbers are always in demand.

HANDY HINT
Many people today are trying to save water in their homes and businesses. If you're thinking about becoming a plumber, it's worth finding out about green plumbing products, such as water-efficient toilets and aerated water-saving shower heads, which use less water than ordinary models.

A plumber positions a pipe. Some plumbers work for building companies, but others are self-employed.

Ruthie: Plumber

"After working for a year with a plumber, I took a two-year part-time course [at a technical college] to learn all aspects of plumbing for water and heating systems. Then I started working as a self-employed plumber.

"I've been working for a few months and gaining experience. I've installed a bath-shower mixer [faucet], repaired leaky [faucets], and replaced the ball valve in toilet cisterns. I've also helped another plumber to install a central heating system. This involved accurately measuring out pipe and cutting it to fit.

"It can be a bit boring at first because sometimes there isn't much you're able to do—you just bring the tools and watch a lot. It can be stressful while you're learning because if you make a mistake, such as causing a leak, you have to fix it with no extra pay.

"Once you're established, though, plumbing is a reasonable business. People always need plumbers. Clients recommend you to their friends, and then you get more work. It's a varied job, too, with lots of problem-solving. I find it very satisfying.

"If you're thinking about becoming a plumber, I'd say that if you're very handy and know something about plumbing already, you could go straight into a job. But if you don't have experience, I'd advise you to [take techincal classes] first to become qualified."

DRYWALLERS AND PLASTERERS

Drywall installing and plastering are other skilled interior jobs. Drywall installers hang and finish new walls (today, usually made from drywall, which consists of a thin layer of gypsum between two layers of heavy paper). Plasterers repair old-fashioned plaster walls or create new ones by mixing and applying plaster to surfaces.

There are two types of drywall workers: installers and finishers. The installers fasten the sheets of drywall to the inside of houses or other buildings. The finishers, or tapers, apply tape to joints, then trowel a joint compound over them to prepare the panels for painting or wallpapering. Drywall and plastering work is mostly indoors, although plastering can also take place on outside walls.

TO BECOME A DRYWALL INSTALLER, YOU WILL NEED
●
to be physically fit
●
good manual skills
●
to work quickly
●
math skills

ORNAMENTAL PLASTERING

This specialized job involves making or repairing decorative plaster moldings, such as ceiling roses or cornices. The plaster is reinforced with short lengths of fiber to hold it together. Some artistic ability is useful in this line of work.

Some general skills are useful for all plasterers. You'll require good coordination and math skills to calculate the quantities of plaster needed. It's vital to be able to work quickly, yet accurately—plaster dries fast!

A plasterer smooths plaster over the ceiling in a new home. Plastering is a messy business. If they're working in an occupied building, plasterers must leave the workspace clean and tidy when they complete the job.

MAIN TASKS: DRYWALL INSTALLER AND FINISHER

●

advising clients on suitable products

●

installing drywall

●

mixing joint compound and applying it

●

sanding the finished compound

●

cleaning up after the job

A specialized plastering job: These plasterers are restoring ornate plasterwork to its former beauty.

WORKING CONDITIONS

Even if you're a drywall installer working mostly indoors, it can be cold if the workplace is an unfinished building. You'll need to work on ladders and possibly on scaffolding, so comfort with heights is helpful. Physical fitness is important, too, because you'll be on your feet or kneeling down for most of the day. Sometimes you'll need to wear protective gear, such as a helmet. As a drywall installer, you'll move from site to site to work and may need to live away from home for some of the time.

ECO-FRIENDLY PLASTERING

As in all areas of construction, some people are seeking more eco-friendly ways of working. For example, new types of plaster have been developed that are made from natural materials and have insulating properties. They help to prevent heat loss through the walls in cold regions; in hot regions, they reduce heat gain. Keeping up with new technologies like these will help you stay ahead of the game.

PAINTERS AND PAPERHANGERS

Are you creative and skillful with your hands? If so, this job could be for you. As a painter and paperhanger, you use paint or wallpaper to protect walls and ceilings and make them look attractive. You could be working in homes, institutions, or factories.

You'll work with various tools, such as brushes and rollers. As well as having good manual skills, you need "people" skills for communicating with clients, math skills for calculating the quantities of materials, and an appreciation of shape and color.

Painting may sound fun, but remember that you will have to do a lot of work preparing the surfaces first. As with other interior jobs, you'll often find yourself working in awkward positions and on ladders. Yet it's a rewarding job, too—you add the final touches to a building and see the job completed.

SPECIAL PAINT JOBS

Some painters and decorators have specialized jobs. They may undertake restoration work on old buildings, such as churches, to restore them to their traditional look. Others specialize in using eco-friendly paints, which do not contain substances that are harmful to the environment. They may also be safer for the painters who work with them and for the people who inhabit the building.

Painters painting a room: One man uses a roller to cover large surfaces, while his colleague uses a brush to ensure a neat finish around the vent.

WHERE WILL I BE?

It takes several years to become a qualified electrician, plumber, plasterer, or painter, whether you're learning purely on the job or studying part time. Once you're experienced, you can decide whether to take the plunge and establish your own business. If you're successful, you can often make more money this way.

Simon: Painter

"I've been a [painter] and builder for 21 years. I found my first job at an employment center—it involved painting a hotel. I didn't have any qualifications or experience, but learned on the job. During the early years of my career, I gained a qualification in hard landscaping, for building patios. Now I'm self-employed, and I mostly do painting work.

"I usually work from 8 a.m. to around 4:30 or 5 p.m., depending on the season and the amount of daylight. In the summer months, I can work longer hours. There's plenty of variety in this line of work. I could be high up on scaffolding, painting the exterior of a building, or indoors painting woodwork.

"I also enjoy meeting different people and seeing their satisfaction when I've finished, and the building looks greatly improved. The disadvantages are mostly to do with being self-employed, such as not having paid vacation time. Sometimes the work is boring, if you're doing exactly the same kind of painting for a long time.

"I'd advise anyone who's interested in this job to find a good place to train. Doing an apprenticeship is ideal. Working on a large building site is great because it offers you opportunities to try out different kinds of work. Builders are [fun] to work with, too!"

This painter is covering furniture and trim before spraying paint to prevent any damage.

Behind the Scenes

Planning and organizing a construction job is a major feat. Here's where the technical people come in—the site inspectors, buyers, estimators, and equipment mechanics that make sure the project runs smoothly. If you're technically minded, there could be something here for you.

There are technicians for every stage of a construction job. For instance, if you're a roofing contractor, you're in charge of planning the construction of the roof. This includes estimating costs, scheduling, and drafting plans and drawings. You'll work with everyone else on the roofing team. Once the job is under way, you'll survey the construction site and supervise the work.

As a technician, you may work in the site office or in a separate location, depending on the job. You'll mostly work a normal workweek, although sometimes there may be overtime when there's a rush to complete a project.

INSPECTORS

Inspectors help with the safety of a building site and make sure construction complies with building codes. To do this job, you need to know about building materials and methods, and health and safety. It's essential to be a skilled organizer.

FINDING A JOB
Construction and building inspectors should have a thorough knowledge of construction practices. Most employers require a high school diploma, and they often look for people who have studied architecture or engineering, or who have a degree from a technical college with courses in building inspection or related fields. In general, much of their training is received on the job from experienced inspectors. Most inspectors are employed by local governments or architectural or engineering services firms.

This inspector uses special equipment to monitor air pollution at a building site.

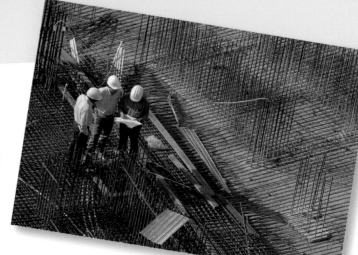

A building site is inspected at every stage to ensure that the job is being carried out according to the specifications.

Anthony: Site Manager

"I've been training as a site [manager] for three years. I started without any experience, but I am learning on the job. I work for a civil engineering company and attend college once a week to earn my degree.

"I work in the site office for 9 to 10 hours a day. Most of my work involves ensuring the drawings are set out properly so the construction workers know the height, dimensions, and position of the structure they're working on. I also [keep] site [logs] and progress records.

"The tasks vary depending on the job—there are different methods for each one. I've worked on a cliff stabilization project and bridge construction. Recently, we had to stabilize a railway line; there was a slope above and below it, and we had to prevent any movement of the line by laying down piles.

"The jobs are scattered, so I usually have to work away from home from Monday to Friday. That's quite difficult, but I've become used to it.

"If you're considering a technical position, it's worth taking a job and studying at the same time. You have to spend much of your free time studying, but you'll learn fast and become qualified quickly."

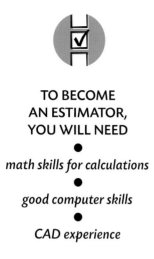

**TO BECOME
AN ESTIMATOR,
YOU WILL NEED**
●
math skills for calculations
●
good computer skills
●
CAD experience

Inspectors check the progress of a project. The original estimates for the budget and schedule for a project sometimes prove inaccurate and have to be revised.

NUMBER CRUNCHING: ESTIMATORS AND BUYERS

If you are good with numbers, you could be an estimator or a buyer. Estimators work out the total cost of the building job and how long it will take. Buyers examine the design drawings to see which materials and services are needed. They then purchase everything that is needed for the project from building suppliers. To do this, they contact suppliers to find the best prices and arrange the delivery of materials when they're needed.

An estimator figures out how much a building project will cost. This includes building materials and the cost of labor and equipment. Estimators need computer skills to use accounting software.

COMPUTERS AND COMMUNICATIONS

For technician jobs, you'll probably be using computer-aided design (CAD) to produce drawings, so excellent computer skills are essential. It's important to be an efficient organizer so that you can meet deadlines. You'll require communications skills for working with suppliers, site workers, and managers.

MAIN TASKS: CAD OPERATOR

●

discussing the brief with the team leader

●

working from existing drawings or models

●

using modeling software to make 2-D and 3-D drawings of a structure

●

using your designs to help prepare estimates of the project costs

A CAD operator works on the design for a chemical factory. If you'd prefer a desk job in the construction industry, this could be for you.

HANDY HINT
Working as a CAD operator might suit you if you'd prefer to work in an office in a quiet environment. You'll spend most of your time in front of a computer and will need to concentrate hard to produce accurate computer models.

CAD OPERATOR
You can get a job purely working on CAD. This involves using computer software to create accurate drawings on the screen to prepare a construction job. You could be working on the designs for houses, factories, or bridges. It helps to have an interest in design and some knowledge of construction methods. For this role, you'll be office-based, working normal office hours, although you may be asked to do overtime at busy times.

At an entry level, the job may be rather repetitive and routine— you could be working on drawings for small components or sections of a project. Once you have more experience, you'll have greater responsibility for the overall design of a project.

With experience, mechanics may advance to field service jobs, where they have a greater opportunity to tackle problems independently. Field positions may require a commercial driver's license and a clean driving record. Technicians with administrative ability may become shop supervisors or service managers. Some technicians open their own repair shops.

A paving machine is used for a road construction project. Equipment mechanics play an important role in maintaining construction machinery.

EQUIPMENT MECHANIC

Enjoy fixing machines? You could be an equipment mechanic. You'll need to complete heavy equipment mechanic training after high school, though some learn on the job. Your job will include servicing, maintaining, and repairing equipment on site or in a workshop. If a machine breaks down, you'll be called in to diagnose the problem. Then you'll have to fix or replace the broken part and put the machine back together again. You'll test it to ensure it's safe for use.

You could be repairing massive machines such as cranes, dump trucks, excavators, or demolition equipment. You'll work on the engines and electronics as well as parts such as the wheels and tracks. For example, you might need to replace the digging arm of an excavator. You will use various kinds of power and hand tools, including cutting and welding equipment. Since most modern machines have electronic components, you'll be trained to use electronic equipment to check for problems.

WET, MUDDY, AND COLD

You'll be working in all weather conditions on a dirty building site and perhaps even underground or at a great height. You'll need to be physically fit to cope with lifting equipment. Although you'll work a normal workweek, you may have to work overtime.

Working as an equipment mechanic can be a risky job. These workers high above the ground are assembling a crane.

Darren: Equipment Mechanic

"I've been fixing machines for 21 years. I took a job with a commercial garage, and I studied part-time for two years to [become qualified] as a mechanic. Eleven years ago, I switched to big [equipment].

"My job varies from day to day. I deal with breakdowns as well as routine service and maintenance. Tomorrow I'll be taking the track apart on a digger and putting on new seals to keep it tight. No two days are the same, so I never get bored.

"Sometimes I work extremely long hours. Construction workers need their machines up and running by the time they start work at 7 a.m. Recently I had to leave home at 4 a.m. to repair some dump trucks on site—exhausting! It's a satisfying job, though. You might have eight machines backed up because of one broken one. You fix it, and people can get back to work.

"If you'd like to be an [equipment] mechanic, I'd suggest becoming an apprentice for a dealership—a company specializing in one brand of machinery, such as [Case] or Caterpillar. The company trains you to its specifications. Modern machines are computerized. You plug in your laptop to diagnose problems and check the fault code. So computer skills are important. It's also hazardous working with large machines, and you must be conscious of health and safety at all times."

Top Jobs

In the construction industry, you can work your way up to a senior management or professional job, for instance, as an architect or a civil engineer, surveyor, or project manager. To achieve this, you need a college degree or equivalent vocational certification, as well as relevant work experience.

TO BECOME
AN ARCHITECT,
YOU WILL NEED
●
to be creative
●
excellent verbal communication skills
●
work experience
●
a professional degree in architecture

ARCHITECT

Architects design new buildings and the space around them, and help to restore old buildings. They are involved with a construction project from start to finish. Architects have to consider how new buildings can be sustainable and need to follow developments in building technologies.

As an architect, your main tasks will include researching the sites that are to be developed, proposing designs to clients, producing technical drawings showing what the buildings will look like, and checking progress once the job is under way. You'll mostly be office based, but will make visits to the site—you'll certainly need to travel for work.

An architect works on a scale model of a building. As well as being good at drawing, architects need to be able to work in 3-D.

To become an architect, you have to study for several years and undertake training in an architect's office. You'll require computer skills in order to use CAD in your work. It's important to enjoy drawing to make detailed designs, and you'll need good communication skills to present your ideas to your clients. You'll need to be an excellent self-organizer to stick to deadlines.

Architects make site visits to check that a building is going according to plan.

Claire: Architect

"I've been an architect for 20 years. It took me seven years to qualify. I studied for a [bachelor's] degree in architectural design and a [master's degree] in architecture, and took an exam to [become licensed]. My training also included two years of work experience. For the last seven years, I've been running my own practice from home. My husband works for me, and when we're busy, we [hire] temporary staff.

"In the mornings, I meet clients, make site visits and have planning meetings, do some drawings, and catch up with administrative tasks. I look after my children after school, and then start work again at 8 p.m. I continue with the drawing work, often until midnight. It's great helping people to design their dream home, and I love working from home and being my own boss.

"The hours are extremely long, though, and I never get away from work. Clients call me at any time, even on weekends. I also have to keep up with my professional obligations, such as attending professional development events.

"If you're thinking about becoming an architect, bear in mind that it takes a long time to qualify and that in times of economic recession, architects are some of the first professionals to lose their jobs. But it can be great fun, and there are many opportunities to work abroad if you're adventurous."

The construction of the Colorado River Bridge. When this five-year project is completed in late 2010, the bridge will span the Black Canyon.

CIVIL ENGINEER

Whenever there's a big civil engineering project, such as a tunnel, wind farm, road, or airport, civil engineers will be there to see the project through. They are involved from the beginning and through to its completion. Consulting engineers advise on the design of projects, while contracting engineers are involved throughout the construction process or help to maintain the structure once it is built.

Consulting engineers investigate the site for construction and prepare feasibility reports to check whether the plans are practical. They help to put together proposals and develop the designs, and they may be responsible for approving the project drawings. Then they work with the contracting engineers to begin implementing the plans.

The contracting engineers schedule the work and supervise the project, dealing with the architects and building workers. They also communicate with the clients, keeping them updated on progress.

STRUCTURAL ENGINEER

Structural engineers play another important role in project design. Working alongside architects, structural engineers check how a building will stand up to the loads and stresses on it. They visit the site during construction to make sure the plans are being followed properly.

MAIN TASKS: STRUCTURAL ENGINEER

●

investigating ground conditions

●

calculating the loads and stresses on buildings

●

testing computer models to ensure the structure can withstand great forces, for example, strong winds

●

checking that the design is followed

Lucía: Civil Engineer

"I'm a qualified civil engineer and have been working in my current job for a construction company for 10 years. I work in an office producing the plans for construction projects. This involves planning the mechanical installations (the heating, plumbing, and fire [safety] systems) and making the necessary calculations. I write reports that define how the installation will be carried out. I draw up plans, which are then passed on to the technical drawing team for completion.

"I work from 8 a.m. until 4 p.m. with a half-hour lunch break. My day is short because I have a young daughter. The others in my team work until 7 p.m. with an hour and a half for lunch. Sometimes I have to bring work home to complete in the evening.

"We're particularly frantic during the last few days before a deadline when we need to deliver the project, and everyone has to put in long hours. On the whole, though, I enjoy the job because I'm always learning new things. I love going past a building knowing that I helped to design it.

"I'd definitely recommend becoming a civil engineer. It's hard work while you're [in college], but your efforts will pay off in the end."

Civil engineers and surveyors use instruments such as this theodolite to make precise measurements of angles for road and tunnel building and other civil engineering projects.

SURVEYING THE SCENE

Surveyors analyze survey data so they can advise on the positioning of a new structure. It's the surveyors who make sure that bridges or pipework are located in the safest place possible.

As a surveyor, you could be responsible for surveying any kind of structure on land or water, either man-made or natural. On land, you could be a building surveyor, advising on all aspects of the design and maintenance of new and existing buildings. You might be a property surveyor, working for people who are buying, selling, or developing properties. Alternatively, you could be working offshore as a marine surveyor. Maybe you'll be mapping the depth of the oceans to provide information for navigation, or aiding the search for much-needed oil or gas resources.

Some surveying jobs are concerned with protecting the environment and using resources efficiently. For example, environmental surveyors advise on ways of minimizing the negative effects of new structures on the environment. They look at ways of making existing buildings more energy efficient.

**TO BECOME
A SURVEYOR,
YOU WILL NEED**

●

*an interest in buildings,
landscape, and
the environment*

●

good computer skills

●

excellent communication skills

Construction surveyors are responsible for overseeing construction projects. They use various types of technical equipment and computers.

Town planners work to improve transportation systems. Here, concrete lining segments for the Channel Tunnel Rail Link are loaded onto a work train. This major construction project, completed in 2007, provided a high-speed rail link from London to the British end of the Channel Tunnel.

MAIN TASKS: TOWN PLANNER

●

using CAD or other computer systems to make models of the proposed development

●

analyzing the effect of the development on a site

●

writing reports for local councils

●

presenting planning proposals at public meetings

●

negotiating between groups with opposing interests

MAKING PLANS

Just like with surveying, many kinds of planning jobs exist. You could be planning anything from house expansions to major structures, such as stations or bridges. Town planners work with local governments to plan new urban developments, for example, shopping centers or sports facilities. They attend meetings with local government officials and local people to discuss the plans and consider the wider impact of the facility, including the transportation options.

Town planners are involved in transportation planning in general. They have to determine how to deal with growing transportation requirements in cities often not built for large volumes of traffic. The planners may consider the improvement of rail networks as well as roads.

Town planners often need to negotiate between groups with different interests. For instance, a local council may support plans to build a new airport to create jobs and expand economic opportunities in the region. However, environmental campaigners may oppose it because it will lead to an increase in carbon dioxide emissions. Emotions run high, and people become angry if the decision does not go their way. It's up to the planners to find a balance between the various interests.

A building developer and construction foreman examine the plans for a high-rise construction project.

MANAGING CONSTRUCTION

Construction projects involve large numbers of people and vast quantities of supplies. It's up to the management team to organize them all.

CONSTRUCTION MANAGERS

At the top level, the construction manager has overall responsibility for a construction job—this could involve coordinating a massive project, such as building an Olympic stadium, with thousands of workers. As construction manager, you're in charge of planning and managing the entire job, keeping to the schedule and the budget, and ensuring all the workers follow health and safety regulations. It's essential to understand legislation related to construction, such as building regulations and planning laws. You must also keep up with changes in the industry, such as new environmental protection laws, and ensure your company complies with them.

TO BECOME A CONSTRUCTION MANAGER, YOU WILL NEED

●

the ability to work under pressure

●

the ability to multitask

●

leadership skills

●

proficiency in oral and written communication skills

WHERE WILL I BE?

There are many advancement opportunities for construction managers. Within large firms, managers may eventually become top-level managers or executives. Very experienced individuals may become independent consultants, while others establish their own construction management services, specialty contracting, or general contracting firm.

GENERAL CONTRACTOR

The next level down from construction manager is the general contractor. In this role, you make sure work on site runs smoothly and deal with any problems. You are in charge of making sure all the materials are available at the right time and within the budget. You organize the labor force so that you have the workers you need on site at the right time. You might be based in an on-site office or in a separate office. Wherever you work, you'll need to make regular site visits to check that the project is going according to plan. As well as a detailed knowledge of the construction industry, you'll need project management skills; computer skills to run software packages to plan the workflow; math skills to ensure you stick to the budget; and excellent communications skills to work with other professionals involved in the project.

FACILITIES MANAGER

This is the person who keeps a building well-maintained once it's built. You'll employ people in the building trade such as electricians and plumbers to work for you as necessary.

The Olympic stadium building site in east London is under construction for the 2012 Olympics. The role of construction manager for a large-scale project like this is one of the top jobs in the industry.

MAIN TASKS: CONSTRUCTION MANAGER

●

checking the project plans with surveyors and architects

●

creating a schedule for the project

●

hiring people to do the work

●

organizing the delivery of building supplies

●

checking progress and sorting out problems

●

communicating with the client

Further Information

BOOKS

Eberts, Marjorie, and Margaret Gisler. *Careers for Hard Hats and Other Construction Types.* McGraw-Hill, 2009.

Harvey, Bethany. *Careers in Construction.* Pearson/Prentice Hall, 2006.

Patterson, David. *Getting a Job in Architecture and Design.* W.W. Norton, 2008.

Sumichrast, Michael, and David Davitaia. *Opportunities in Building Construction Careers.* McGraw-Hill, 2008.

Waldrep, Lee. *Becoming an Architect: A Guide to Careers in Design.* John Wiley & Sons, 2010.

WEB SITES

www.archcareers.org
Do you want to be an architect? This web site will give you an overview of the varied and diverse paths to a career in architecture and the steps required to get there.

www.architects.org
The web site of the Boston Society of Architects offers advice and resources for those interested in a career in architecture.

www.bls.gov/oco
For hundreds of different types of jobs in the construction field, the Occupational Outlook Handbook gives information on education needed, earnings, job prospects, and more.

www.careeroverview.com/construction-careers.html
This site offers an overview of careers in construction, training and job qualifications, employment opportunities, and earnings information.

www.constructionjobs.com
The nation's premier employment job board and resume database for the construction, design, and building industries.

Glossary

apprenticeship a training program that allows apprentices to work for money, learn a trade, and become qualified

asphalt a mixture containing a sticky black substance called bitumen, used for making the surface of roads and for roofing

building regulations government rules to ensure that buildings are designed and constructed safely

ceiling rose the circular fitting on a ceiling used for attaching a light

computer-aided design (CAD) a software program that allows the user to create computer-generated drawings to prepare information for a construction project

conservation protection of a building of special architectural value

contractor a person or company that has a contract to do work for another company

cornice a decorative band of wood designed to hide curtain fixtures

dealership a business established to sell or distribute a company's goods or services in a particular area

dormer a vertical window made in the sloping roof of a house

drywall a building material made of sheets of paper with gypsum between them, used for interior walls and ceilings

drywalling attaching "dry" plasterboard to walls and ceilings rather than a "wet" plaster finish

emissions polluting waste products, such as carbon dioxide, that are released into the atmosphere

formwork temporary wood structures used to contain fresh concrete until it is strong enough to support itself

geothermal energy system a system using heat from underground, such as a heat pump

heavy equipment heavy machines, such as cranes and diggers, used on building sites

insulate to protect a building with a material that prevents heat from passing through

jigsaw a tool with a fine blade for cutting designs in pieces of metal or wood

joiner a person who makes the wooden parts of the building, such as doors

joist a long, thick piece of wood or metal used to support a floor or ceiling in a building

level a glass tube partly filled with liquid, with a bubble of air inside. It is used to test whether a surface is level; if the bubble is in the center, then the surface is level.

pile a type of foundation that is driven deep into the ground

restoration repairing and cleaning an old building to make its condition as good as it was originally

roof sheeting a lightweight covering made from metal, plastic, or a type of cement and attached to the roof

sander an electric tool with a rough surface used to make wood smooth

solar energy energy from the heat of the sun

subcontract to pay a person or company to do some of the work that you have been contracted to do

surveyor a person who examines a structure to check its condition or to examine or record the details of a piece of land or underwater structure

sustainable a building that is constructed and can be used with minimal resources so it creates little waste and does not harm people or the environment

telescopic forklift a forklift truck with a telescopic boom (long arm), which can lift heavier loads and has a longer range than other forklifts

ventilate to allow fresh air to enter and move around a building

welding joining pieces of metal together by heating their edges and pressing them together

Index